812   Childress, Alice   c.1

When the rattlesnake
sounds

DATE			
NOV 4 '77	NOV 8'	NOV - 6 2000	
MAY 1 2 '78	MAR 2 9 '81	NOV 9 2003	
JUN 9 '78	NOV 23 '81	MAR 1 2	
JAN 8 '82	MAY 0 '92		
NOV 26 '85	OCT 1 6 '92		
NOV 24 '86	NOV 2 0 '92		
MAY 5 '87	APR 27 '93		
FEB 23 1989	OCT -7 '93		
SEP 26 '89	NOV 21 '94		
SEP 2 3 '90	APR 2 6 '95		

When the
Rattlesnake Sounds

When the Rattlesnake Sounds

a play by ALICE CHILDRESS
drawings by Charles Lilly

Coward, McCann & Geoghegan, Inc.

New York

SBN: GB-698-30594-9
SBN: TR-698-20342-9
Library of Congress Catalog Card Number: 75-10456

PRINTED IN THE UNITED STATES OF AMERICA / 12 up

designed by Cathy Altholz

812
C.1

Remembering
my mother, Florence
and her sisters
Gertrude, Lorraine, and Vera

HARRIET TUBMAN

was born the slave of Edward Brodas in Maryland about 1821. She died March 10, 1913, in Auburn, New York. She fully felt the indignities and cruelty of slavery, suffering beatings, injuries and working as a field hand under subhuman conditions. When she reached womanhood, she dreamed of running North to free territory. She took others with her when she went, then returned many times to rescue more than three hundred Black men, women, and children . . . by way of the Underground Railroad, a route made up of secret paths and hiding places in the homes of those who wanted slavery abolished. She spent her life as an Underground Conductor and also earned money to contribute to the funds raised by abolitionists for food, medicine, clothing, etc. needed for the rescue work. One summer she worked as a laundress in a hotel at Cape May, New Jersey. This fact inspired the author to write the following play which is fictional but based upon Harriet Tubman's true feelings, as expressed by her many times, concerning commitment and fear.

TIME:

Very close to the end of legal slavery.

PLACE:

Cape May, New Jersey.

SCENE:

A hotel laundry room.

CHARACTERS

HARRIET TUBMAN /
An experienced leader who knows how to handle people with firmness . . . and love. Actually she was a little woman, five feet tall, but for the purposes of a play the qualities of leadership and compassion are more important than actual appearance. She is in her early forties.

LENNIE /
A strong, determined, no-nonsense kind of young woman. She is used to hard work and is perhaps physically stronger than Harriet, but does not have the tact to handle leadership. She is about twenty-five years old.

CELIA /
A very attractive young woman who has certainly been more sheltered than the other two. Celia is also a dedicated person . . . but she sees the freedom struggle in romantic terms . . . and has the tendency to get fed up when the going is grubby and ordinary.

There is a pile of loose laundry on the floor waiting to be done . . . much with flounces and lace to suggest the summer clothing of ladies in the 1860's. There are three washtubs filled with water and laundry; in each tub is a washboard. Harriet, Lennie, and Celia are washing clothes. The women are dressed in calico dresses and aprons. Harriet and Lennie work vigorously, absorbed in the task. Celia is slowing up and finally stops.

CELIA
(Cautiously watching Harriet and Lennie.)
Lord, I'm tired. *(Others keep working.)* Seem like we workin way past our dinnertime, don't it? Harriet? Lennie?

LENNIE
Not much past dinner. It feels like about one o'clock.

HARRIET
We're gonna stop an eat by 'n by. We'll put out five bundles of wash today. Yesterday was only four.

CELIA
Only four? When I went to bed last night, I cried, I was so bone-weary. Only? How can four bundles of wash be *only*?

HARRIET
Just a while longer, Celia. Let's sing. When you singin, the work goes fast. You pick a song, Lennie.

LENNIE
(Decides to pick one that will annoy Celia.)
Wadin in the water, wadin in the water (children)

Wadin in the water, God gonna trouble the water.

(*Harriet joins her in singing.*)

CELIA

(*Drying her hands on her apron.*)
I want my dinner now. I'm hungry.

LENNIE

We all hungry, Celia. Can't you hold out a little more?

CELIA

If we *all* hungry, why don't we *all* eat? We been up since seven this mornin . . . workin. For what? Why?

LENNIE

You know why! We got to finish five bundles.

CELIA

(*To the heavens above.*)
Five bundles for what?

LENNIE

For a dollar and a quarter, that's what! (*Grumbling.*) I'm tellin you . . . some people.

HARRIET

(*Sensing trouble, she stops washing.*)
Celia is right, Lennie. It's not good to kill yourself workin.

LENNIE
(In anger.)
She knows why we're doin it, Harriet. Some people . . . I'm tellin you.

HARRIET
(Firmly.)
Let's have our dinner Lennie.

LENNIE
(Her eyes on Celia.)
Did you fix it again, Harriet? We suppose to take turns. I take a turn, you take a turn, then . . . .

HARRIET
(Hastily cutting her off.)
I got some nice corn bread and some side meat. The coffee should be ready.
(Handing out paper parcels to the girls.)
We need to rest awhile. Here, Celia, and that's yours, Lennie."
(Going back to her tub.)
I'll just wash out these few more pieces before my water turns cold.

LENNIE
I ain't restin unless you rest too. Not like some people I know.

CELIA
She keep sayin *some people.* Wonder who she means?

14

HARRIET
(With a sigh.)
I'll stop too.

CELIA
*(Looking at the pile of unwashed clothes
as she unwraps her lunch.)*
White folks love white clothes and they love to
sit in the grass too . . . and I'm sick of scrubbin
grass stains.

HARRIET
Well, we need the money.

CELIA
*(Puts down her lunch and snatches
up a flouncy white dress.)*
Look at all the money *they* got. This cost every
bit of twelve dollars. *(Imitating the hotel guests.)*
Spendin the summer in a big hotel, ridin round
in carriages. *(Drops her airy act and goes back to
anger.)* If just one of em give us what she spend
in a week . . . we wouldn't have to work two
months in no hotel laundry.

LENNIE
I got a life-size picture of them givin you that
much money. They ain't gonna give you nothin,
so you better be glad you got the chance to *earn*
some.

CELIA

Scrubbin! Ain't that a damn somethin to be glad about? Excuse me, Harriet, I meant to say dern or drat.

HARRIET

Celia got somethin on her mind, and she need to talk, so let her talk, Lennie. But no dammin, dernin, or drattin either. All here got more manners than to cuss.

LENNIE

(As she looks at Harriet's food.)
Is that your dinner? You ain't got no meat on your bread, Harriet.

HARRIET

I don't too much like meat.

LENNIE

I know who do. Some people.

CELIA

(Bursting out at Harriet.)
Stop sayin that! You do too like meat! Stop makin out like you don't. You goin without so you can save another nickel. Yall drivin me outta my head. Maybe I'm just not suited for this kinda thing.

LENNIE

But I am, huh?

HARRIET
(Quietly and seriously.)
You tired of this bargain we made? You sorry about it and don't know how to quit?

LENNIE
(Flaring with anger.)
She promised and she got to stick by it! Your father is a *deacon of the church* . . . and if you don't keep your word, you gonna bring disgrace down on him and *every member* of your family.

HARRIET
Lennie, don't be so brash. Mother and father is one thing . . . child is another. Each one stands upon his own deeds. She don't have to stay. Celia, you can go if you want.

CELIA
I don't really want to get out of it. But I want *some* of my money for myself. I'm tired of sleepin three in a room. I want to spend a little of the money . . . just a little, Harriet. Buy a few treats.

LENNIE
She's jealous of them rich white ladies . . . cause they got silk parasols to match they dresses. I heard her say it. "Wish I had me a silk parasol."

HARRIET
We eatin and sleepin. We spend for that and nothin more . . . that was the bargain.

CELIA
(To Lennie.)
I could own a silk parasol *and* carry it . . . without actin like a field hand.

HARRIET
I been a field hand, children. Harness to a plow like a workhorse.

CELIA
Scuse me, I'm sorry.

LENNIE
(Really sarcastic.)
Celia, that don't sound nothin like them big speeches you used to make in church meetin. *(Mocking Celia.)* "I'll die for my freedom!" . . . Had everybody whoopin and hollerin every time you open your mouth, whole church stompin and shoutin amen.

CELIA
(Sadly.)
I remember how it was.

(The women remove their aprons and Harriet takes her place center stage. Church music in from off-stage tape or recording of "The Old Ship of Zion", or any of the A. M. E. Zion songs. Harriet Tubman was a member of that church. She addresses the audience as though they are the congregation.)

HARRIET

(Music and humming are in low as she speaks.)
God bless you, brothers and sisters, bless you,
children.

OFFSTAGE VOICES PLUS LENNIE AND CELIA

Amen . . . Amen . . . Bless God.

HARRIET

I thank the good Lord for the support of the
African Methodist Episcopal Zion Church in the
freedom struggle. There is comfort and good
fellowship here.

CHURCH VOICES

Yes, Lord. Amen.

HARRIET

Not like hidin in the bitter cold, with the huntin
dogs followin you down with no restin place in
sight. We had to give the little babies paregoric
so they wouldn't cry and let the paddy-rollers
know where to find us. We crossed some lonely
roads and rivers . . . the dark of the night
around us, the clouds cuttin off the sight of the
North Star. But everything was all right cause
where I go . . . God goes . . . and I carry a gun
. . . two guns . . . a hand pistol and a shoulder
rifle . . . just in case the Lord tell me I got to use
it!

CHURCH VOICES
Amen! Speak! Praise the holy name! Amen!

HARRIET
I thank the Father for the help and assistance of the Society of Friends and the abolitionists, and all well-wishers.

CHURCH VOICES
Amen, Amen, Amen.

HARRIET
But as I put my hand to the plow to do the work of Freedom, so I also put *my money* into the work. I have none now, so I will spend my summer washin and ironin so that when the fall come I have *some of my own* to put . . . to buy food, medicine, paregoric for the babies, and ammunition for the pistol. . . . Lord grant I never use it. Any ladies here want to go with me to wash clothes and give the money to free our slave brethren?

LENNIE
(Stands by Harriet's side.)
If you would have me, Mrs. Tubman, it would be the greatest honor, a great honor indeed.

HARRIET
Thank you, my daughter.

CELIA
*(Stands up and throws her arms out
in a Joan of Arc gesture.)*
I'll die for my freedom! Take me, Sister! I'm
ready to fight the good fight. Hallelujah!

CHURCH VOICES
(Celia has set the church to rocking.)
Glory! Glory! Hallelujah! Fight the good fight!
Amen!
(Music fades out as women don their aprons again.)

CELIA
I remember how it was, Lennie, and the promise
I made. But how much can we get like this?
Maybe if *everybody* worked and gave their
money to the Underground, it would mean somethin. This way I just can't see it, but I believe in
freedom and I understand.

HARRIET
Ain't no such thing as only "understandin."
Understandin mean action. You have to look
after what *Celia* does . . . and if *nobody else* do
nothin, you got to. Freedom is just a baby, and
you its mother. You don't stop lovin and carin
for it just cause others don't care.

CELIA
Maybe it's easy to talk like that when you

Moses. It's easy to kill yourself for somethin when thousands of people be cheerin you on. Lennie and Celia don't mean nothin to nobody. We could die here and nobody would know or care.

LENNIE
Don't you talk for me! Ain't nothin greater to me than to be able to say . . . "I, Lennie Brown, scrubbed clothes side by side with Moses. " If you lookin for praise, you don't belong here.

HARRIET
Children, let us keep peace. We act like we hate each other worse than we hate the slaveowner.

CELIA
I know what I sound like. . . .
(Falls at Harriet's feet and holds out her hands.)
Oh, Harriet, my hands are skinned sore.

LENNIE
Do, Jesus, look at Celia's hands.

HARRIET
(Turns Celia's head and searches for the truth.)
But it ain't your hands that's really botherin you. It ain't food, it ain't sleepin three in a room, and it ain't about silk parasols. What's botherin you, Celia?

CELIA

I'm so shame for feelin the way I do. Lord knows
I'm shame.

HARRIET

Tell it. Speak your shame.

CELIA

I'm *scared*. If these people in this hotel knew
who you was. Forty thousand dollars' reward
out for you!

LENNIE

*(Dashes to the door to see if anyone
is around to listen.)*
Hush your fool mouth! Moses got the charm.
Slave holder will never catch Moses.

CELIA

I'm so shame. All those other things just lies. I
ain't so terrible tired. I'm just scared and shame
cause I'm afraid. Me talkin so big. Sure, I'd work
all summer and give the money to the Underground. It did sound so good in the meetin
where it was all warm and friendly. Now I'm
scared of gettin into trouble. I never been no
slave. And I'm scared of nothin round me but
white folks.

LENNIE

We ain't got no room for no rabbity, timid kinda
women in this work.

HARRIET

Oh, yes, Lennie, we got room for the timid and
the brave. Poor little Celia. Child, you lookin at
a woman who's been plenty afraid. When the
rattlesnake sounds a warnin . . . it's time to be
scared. Ain't that natural? When I run away was
nobody to cheer me on . . . don't you think I
was scared?

LENNIE

But you got to freedom.

HARRIET

(The feeling of a "meeting" begins.)
Oh, but when I found I'd crossed that line! There
was such a glory over everything. The sun came
shinin like gold through the trees.

LENNIE

(Feels she is at church meeting.)
You felt like you was in heaven! You was free!

HARRIET

But there was no one to welcome me in the land
of freedom. I was a stranger in a strange land.
My home, after all, was down in the old cabin

25

quarters with the ones I knew and loved . . . my slave mother and father, brothers, sisters and friends. Aunt Day . . . she used to be midwife, tend the sick, bury the dead. Two field hands I knew, they used to ease some the work off the women who was expectin. There I was standin on free land, with my heart back down there with them. What good is freedom without your people?

LENNIE

Go on, Harriet!

HARRIET

And so to this solemn resolution I come: As I was free . . . *they* would be free also.

LENNIE

Praise God, that's Harriet Tubman!

HARRIET

Sometimes I was scared in the icy river. Chilled to the bone and just might drown.

LENNIE

But you got cross.

HARRIET

I was scared in the dark and the swamp . . . but I come to the light. Most times I was full of hatred for the white folks.

LENNIE
And you came to the Friends.

HARRIET
And I came to John Brown.
*(Offstage music . . . soft violin . . . sound of
voices ad-libbing at a reception.)*
There was this big, fine affair, A reception.
Abolitionist reception. The ladies were all
dressed in lovely gowns, made by free labor. I
was in my best too . . . but that wasn't too much
better than what I'm standin in. They had pretty
cakes and a punch bowl . . . the grandest party.
Violin music . . . what you call elegant. There
was a goodly crowd, and I was way on the other
side of the room, away from the main door
where the people would enter. Everybody
called him Captain Brown . . . Captain.

*(Harriet moves to the far side of the stage and turns
toward the opposite door to illustrate the distance
between her and Captain Brown.)*

HARRIET
The whisper started way down the hall and came
through the room . . . "It's Captain Brown. He's
here. Captain Brown is about to enter." Then he
came in the door. He was a fine, stern-lookin
gentleman . . . goodness glowed from his face
like a burnin light. The room got quiet. He

looked all around until he saw me. Mind now, we had never met. The ladies and gentlemen were all tryin to meet him. . . . Oh, it was Captain, Captain, Captain. He held up his hand. There was silence, then he said . . . "The first I see is General Tubman. The second is General Tubman. The third is General Tubman." He crossed the room and bowed to me . . . and I shook his hand.

LENNIE
And he died for us, didn't he?

HARRIET
Celia, he was a brave man, but I believe he must have been scared sometimes. But he did what he had to do.

CELIA
I guess he was just brave. Some folks braver than others.

HARRIET
I was with hundreds of brave black men on battleground. I was there, Celia. We saw the lightning and that was the guns, then we heard the thunder and that was the big guns, then we heard the rain falling. . . . And that was the drops of blood. And when we came to get the crops, it was dead men we reaped.

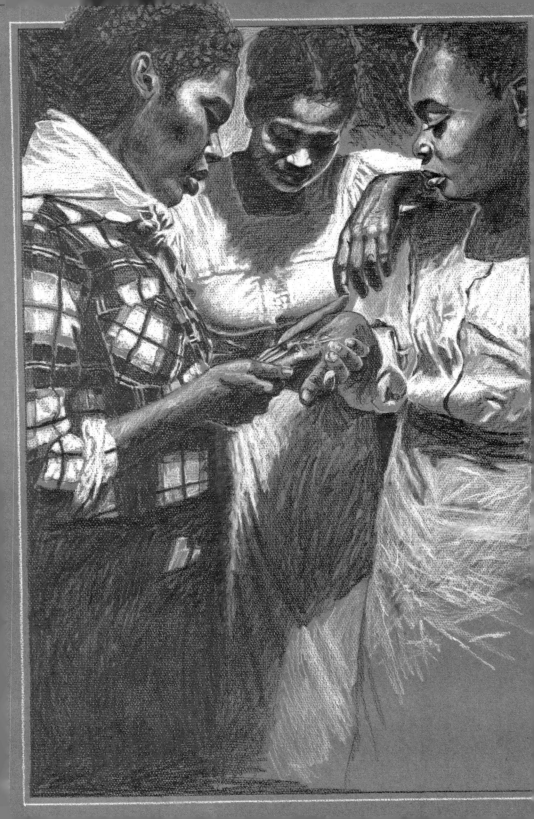

LENNIE

Fightin for us to be free. I guess they musta been scared sometimes.

HARRIET

Give me your hand, Celia. Look, see the skin broken across the knuckles. Counta you some man or woman gonna have warm socks and boots to help em get to freedom. See the cuts the lye soap put in your skin. Counta you some little baby is gonna be born on free soil. It won't matter to him that you was afraid, won't matter that he did not know your name. Won't nothin count ceptin he's free. A livin monument to Celia's work.

(Celia cries.)

You go to the room and rest. Maybe you might want to stay here after you think about it.

LENNIE

Sure, Celia . . . think bout it. We can manage. And if you want to go home, we won't hold it against you. I ought not to have said what I did. Sometimes I get scared myself . . . but it makes me act evil *and* brave, you know?

CELIA

I don't want to go home. Guess there's worse things than fear. I'm glad to know I don't have to be shame about it.

HARRIET

That's right. If you was home doin nothin, what would you have to be fraid bout? That's when a woman oughta feel shame, shame to her very soul.

CELIA

(Gathers up clothes, places them in tub, starts working. Harriet goes to her tub.)
If we sing, the work goes faster.

LENNIE

(Goes to her tub.)
Your time to pick a song, Celia.

CELIA

(Celia starts scrubbing. They all work for a few moments. Celia has decided on a song. She sings out.)
Oh, Lord, I don't feel no ways tired
Children, Oh, Glory Hallelujah
For I hope to shout *Glory* when this world
  is all on fire
Oh, Glory, Hallelujah
(The others join her on the second round.)
Oh, Lord, I don't feel no ways tired. . . .

CURTAIN